HANDBOOK
OF
HOPE

HANDBOOK OF HOPE

First Aid for Surviving the Suicide
of a Loved One

Mary Elizabeth Burgess

authorHOUSE®

AuthorHouse™ LLC
1663 Liberty Drive
Bloomington, IN 47403
www.authorhouse.com
Phone: 1-800-839-8640

Second Edition

Published by AuthorHouse 12/17/2013

ISBN: 978-1-4918-4157-0 (sc)
ISBN: 978-1-4918-4158-7 (e)

Library of Congress Control Number: 2013922428

CONTENTS

Acknowledgments ix

Preface xi

The Emergency Room 1

The Recovery Room 15

Recuperation 31

What readers say about
Handbook of Hope

"This book was a lifesaver for our family after we lost our son to suicide. It contains so much useful and helpful information. The handbook helped us better understand that the pain and heartache we were experiencing were normal and that there is hope for survival."

—Janet Groff, Mother

"In this brief but useful book, Mary Burgess helps bereaved readers to 'say yes to life again' by providing practical advice and helpful suggestions for all aspects of grief: physical, emotional, mental and spiritual. Many will benefit from her work."

—Rita M. Bonchek, Ph.D.,
Grief Therapist

"With empathy and humor, Mary Burgess has written a survival guide for those who have lost a loved one to suicide. I strongly recommend this book to anyone in that unfortunate situation."

—Larien G. Bieber, M.D., F.A.C.P.

"Readily accessible aid for surviving a suicide is well outlined in Handbook of Hope, a testimony to the author's effective and positive use of personal and spiritual resources. As one who has felt her pain and rejoiced in her healing, I can say she has practiced what she has preached."

—Carl J. Frederick, M.Div., Pastor

"Handbook of Hope was very helpful and a good source of information during a difficult time in my life. Death is not always something we understand. But with information that enables us to move on with our lives, we realize there is hope for surviving."

—Rhonda Daniels, Mother

In memory of Tom,

child of God,

who struggled valiantly.

My everlasting thanks:

- to Scott, my son, for technical assistance and encouragement,

- to Debbie, my daughter-in-law, for sharing her heart and for her loyalty, devotion, and support

- to counselors, pastors, physicians, and many friends whose wisdom sustains me,

- to grieving parents who urged publication of this book,

- to Benay for finding the rainbow,

- and most of all, to God without whose love and grace none of the above would be possible, nor my very life.

PREFACE

This survival manual is based on the experience of my family's loss when my son Tom took his life. Tom was beloved as a husband, son, brother and friend. Though the loss had the same cause, Tom's survivors mourned in various ways.

In writing this book, I've drawn on experiences of each of us, including the early death of my uncle who died by his own hand (my first suicide loss) in the 1950's, and my best friend's suicide in 1978. My own victory over depression and suicidal intentions years ago lent valuable direction and insight to my life as well as to this manual.

Surviving the aftermath of your loved one's suicide may be the hardest thing you'll ever do. It will take work, but you won't do it alone. You have family, friends and, hopefully, faith to sustain you. Many are there, ready to reach out to you. Let them.

Everyone reacts to and recovers from any deep loss in their own way and in their own time frame. This book is only a guide to point out some of the ways that may facilitate recovery from the uniquely devastating event of suicide. I urge you to adapt its suggestions to your situation and temperament.

At first **emergency** treatment is essential. As grieving proceeds, you need time to **recover** from shock. Finally, you enter a period of **recuperation** where healing becomes deeper and moves you into true survivorship. You'll find the parts of this manual arranged into these three "stages."

Recognizing that the survivor's concentration and motivation are limited, I've written this handbook in short, action-oriented "bursts," a format intended to offer readily accessible aid. The reader will not be intimidated by long paragraphs of prose.

In spite of being battered and bruised, you may emerge stronger, more caring, and more understanding of the pain of others. You will never *get over* this tragedy, but you can learn to *live with* it.

I truly believe God's hand was guiding mine in writing this manual. I hope you will accept it as God's gift to us, the survivors. God bless.

MEB

THE EMERGENCY ROOM

Expect to feel in shock.

Shock and numbness may last for days, even weeks or months, off and on. You will want this wrenching loss to go away, to wake up to find it was all a nightmare.

You may often re-play the chaos.

Expect to re-live:

- the disintegration of your gut when the first realization hit or when you found your loved one,
- the indignity of emergency vehicles, police and coroner,
- denial, hurt, explanations (any and all that leaped to mind),
- playing a role, being someone else: calm, cool, collected, or hysterical.

It was all a surreal montage in which nothing made sense, only that your world had suddenly exploded.

No doubt you will have trouble sleeping and eating.

Keeping your thoughts together is another problem. You haven't lost your mind—just a very precious person.

If you were the one who found your loved one dead, that image may haunt you for awhile. In time, it will be softened by pleasant images as they surface to your memory from better days.

Ride the roller coaster of emotions.

Many different feelings will overwhelm, one after the other.

It's okay to feel anger, relief, guilt, regret and sorrow too deep for words— but don't act on your feelings if they're destructive.

It's not uncommon to want to join the loved one in death. But if you feel this way, TELL someone.

Let others enter the pain.

They want to help bear your load. You would do the same for them. This is love in its sweetest, most mysterious guise at work.

Talk as much as you need to.

The need to describe your experiences and feelings is a naturally strong one and part of the beginning of healing.

Friends and family may be your best sounding board now. Or contact a trusted clergyman or counselor if you need objective, caring advice.

When you need to withdraw, do so.

Don't ignore your need to ventilate, but, at times you must find a retreat, your own special sanctum, to sob, yell, beat your breast—or just be alone.

It's not unusual if all you feel right now is numb. You can let other feelings back in when it's safer to deal with them.

Crying is good for the soul—and the body.

It's believed tears release some of the body's negative chemicals when it is experiencing pain or stress.

Don't be concerned about what other think. Crying is one of the healthiest ways to vent your feelings.

If you think you'll never stop, remember that you have the rest of your life to weep. You don't have to do it all today, this moment.

Visit your doctor.

Use medication if you really need it, especially to sleep or soothe the stomach, but only temporarily and only with the advice of a physician.

Avoid or reduce usage of other chemicals.

Alcohol, caffeine or nicotine may temporarily numb, but they ultimately interfere with the body's own healing mechanism.

And, of course, NO illegal drugs.

Make extra allowance for yourself.

Especially if this is the first major loss in your life, you will feel in an altered state. Realize that the worst has already happened to you.

Others deeply acquainted with grief may be helpful, but each loss is unique. If what people suggest is not healing, disregard their advice.

On the other hand, try to be open to any suggestions that may ease your distress.

Eat something, even if you haven't an appetite.

But do so gently. Eat small amounts at a time, perhaps more frequently than usual.

The so-called soft foods—gelatin, puddings, bland soups, toast, potatoes, pasta, fruits—are easiest to digest. Avoid fatty and highly seasoned foods, except in wee quantities.

Yes, chicken soup is good for more than the soul.

Allow God's love to fill you, surround you, uplift you.

Such love comes directly, or through the care, concern and prayers of others. Lean into and on it.

Use the words that are comfortable for you.

They may be "committed suicide," "took his life," or, simply, "died." (Committing suicide sounds too much like committing murder—which it is. Your loved one was both victim and killer, an unhappy thought. At some point, you may want to try to understand why this is the most complicated and devastating of griefs.)

In the long run it is not healing to make up a story about accident or illness (other than depression) taking your loved one's life. Be truthful with others and you will be able to be truthful with yourself.

Repeat your story as often as necessary.

Talking makes it real. Eventually, you will not have to re-live every detail.

Ask "Why?" but don't expect answers.

Not yet. Avoid ruminating. Thinking too much results in a cycle of frustration.

Avoid blaming yourself. This act was your loved one's decision, not yours.

If children or teenagers are among the survivors, seek professional help.

Many experts believe suicide is the most devastating death to encounter. Its after-effects on adults, let alone children, can be lifelong. Though they may appear to be handling the grief well now, children and teens can enter a stage of denial from which it is difficult to emerge. They need to be able to talk about the death freely to prevent wounds from causing later emotional problems.

And you need to separate your grief from theirs.

However, if the news is given honestly and sensitively, a child's wisdom may be healing for others. One four-year old, after pondering the news that her father's best friend had died (she'd made a get-well card while he was sick), said simply, "He couldn't live anymore."

The fear you may feel is normal.

You face many unknowns just now. Deal with them one at a time as you are able.

Most problems can be postponed for awhile. When you are able to face things with clearer thinking, you will find people ready to help you through many of the things that now loom over you.

Breathe deeply.

This relieves tension and fills you with a life force. Lie flat, place one hand on your abdomen, the other on your chest.

Let air slowly fill your body so that your abdomen rises. Air will automatically inflate your lungs.

Release the air very slowly and easily. (This is the way babies breathe, totally relaxed.)

Repeat several times, letting tension ooze from the muscles of your arms, your neck and shoulders, your back, your front.

Shame and embarrassment may accompany the mixture of emotions you feel.

This is because the view of society-at-large seems to be that suicide is a cowardly, selfish, even unforgiveable act.

Taking his or her life did not make your loved one a bad person, only a very depressed one.

Understand that *no one* takes his or her own life on a whim. A long and agonizing struggle precedes the act, whether it is for days or months or hours.

In the midst of unfathomable pain, it can take great courage and strength to resolve that struggle whether one decides to end the pain or allow it to continue.

Shock recurs over and over.

Every time you wake up forgetting for a brief moment that something terrible has happened, you get hit in the face the gut, the heart with the awful realization that your loved one is gone, truly gone.

In time, the shock will be replaced by numbness and sorrow that too are part of the process.

Celebrate your loved one's life.

If possible, at the funeral or memorial service have a memoribilia table with pictures and items showing the miracle of this precious life, however long or short it was.

You can invite friends and family to your home for a similar celebration if the service is past. Reminiscing about happier times in your loved one's life can be therapeutic for everyone.

You may want to postpone this event to a later time. However, it will likely be most helpful soon after the death, surely before the first anniversary. (See "Recovery" and "Recuperation.")

Pray, even if you've never prayed before.

If, when you learned of your loved one's suicide, you said, "Oh, my God!" from the depths of your soul, you prayed.

Now, simply ask God for what you need—sleep, peace of mind, support, understanding, comfort—and wait for God to give it to you.

If you can't pray, ask others to pray for you.

THE RECOVERY ROOM

You've had major surgery.

Stay in the recovery room as long as you need to. Alternate periods of rest and activity frequently. Five minutes of rest every hour or two may do more good than a prolonged sleep.

Numbness may alternate with periods of intense emotion.

Reality is sinking down to many levels of consciousness. You may still expect to see your loved one walk in the door, yet you just as surely realize this will never be.

Such awareness brings intense pain and discomfort, perhaps periods of despondency along with confusion, anger, guilt.

In time, the intensity of these feelings will decrease, but by all means seek professional help if your distress continues.

Listen to others.

But don't expect their advice to always fit how you grieve because each person grieves uniquely. Let friends and family know you appreciate their caring and attention.

If they hover, inform them that you need space and time for private healing.

Expect to feel raw for some time.

So many painful feelings are on the surface. It's easy to flare up unintentionally at the slightest provocation.

Cool down, apologize, forgive yourself—whatever it takes to make such incidents less hurtful.

Physical work, for some, is therapeutic.

It diverts attention and releases energy harmlessly. While you are numb emotionally, work may help you feel that you're still alive.

However, if you use work—or anything else—to escape the pain entirely, the healing process may be slower.

Plead your case for adequate time from work, if necessary.

Many employers will consider an extension of leave if you explain the circumstances.

Don't be surprised if your thought processes are erratic. Keep thinking tasks to a minimum as much as possible. No one can predict when, but *normalcy will return.*

Exercise to release nervous tension and to get in touch with your body.

One person found that acute stomach pain dissipated when walking for exercise because the nervous energy was diverted to a more wholesome use. The same thing can happen if anxiety is causing chest tightness, muscle cramps, breathing difficulty, or other somatic symptoms.

Hopefully, your body's been serving you well, but now you have to tend it. Simple stretching exercises for the legs, back, and neck may suffice. Ask a friend to give you a massage.

Walking enables you to feel life in your body again. Walk with your back straight, your shoulders back (pinch your shoulder blades together), your knees slightly bent and loose. Step easily. Breathe deeply.

Having to deal with guilt is inevitable.

When it plagues you (as it does every suicide survivor),
recognize that you alone could not have been the cause of your loved one's death.

If he was getting treatment, even the professionals didn't prevent the suicide. This is not uncommon, especially if the person appeared to be getting better.

Be careful about blaming others.

Whatever culpability exists,

> *no one can be certain,*

about the mix of complex factors that led to your loved one's death.

Also, usually those blamed are other family members. Like you, they are hurting. You need each other's strength now. Don't deplete it by recrimination.

Avoid busy roads when driving.

You haven't lost your driving ability, but now you may need every bit of mental energy to stay focused.

Take the easiest, less traveled route—even if it's not necessarily the shortest—until your concentration begins to return.

Continue breathing.

Deeply.

Allow the world to enter your being through the gift of the senses.

See the beauty around you in people and in nature.

Hear the sounds of life: bird calls, puppies barking, lawn mowers (snow blowers?)

Smell new-mown grass, musky moist earth after a summer rain (or freshly fallen snow).

Feel the wind on your face.

Touch a rose petal, a dog's wiry coat, a baby's skin.

Take comfort that your loved one is at peace.

But acknowledge that you and the other survivors are among the living. Your welfare is paramount now. It's time for you to find peace, too.

You can hate what your loved one's death is doing to you.

But don't hate the person.

Consider journaling.

If you have not yet started to write down your thoughts, buy a pretty blank book or use an ordinary spiral notebook.

You may write only a sentence or two a day. Some days you may write a chapter! Forget spelling, grammar, and punctuation. Just give shape to your feelings and thoughts on paper.

This is a good technique to vent feelings, organize thoughts, and put your troubles into a manageable form and bring them "down to size."

Such writing will also, in time, provide markers for yourself for signs of progress.

Try on "normal."

It's not irreverent to talk about matters other than this tragedy. You will want and need to visit and re-visit it often, but trips into the "normal world" are healthy.

If doubts recur about your loved one's soul, speak to a member of the clergy.

An old myth persists, based on medieval church teaching meant to discourage suicide, that a suicide victim could not enter heaven because he could not repent of his "sin" after committing it and thus would not be able to be forgiven. Some early Christians were choosing suicide as a way to enter God's kingdom before natural death.

Today most churches teach God as just and loving and therefore reject that early belief. Don't let ancient teachings torment you.

Include humor in your recovery plan.

Laughter exercises the lungs and provides more than "comic relief." You're not weird for laughing at such a solemn time in your life.

Please keep breathing.

Get mad at a Higher Power if you want.
He or She can handle it.

You can't have a relationship of depth with that Higher Power unless you are honest. But don't be angry with yourself. Yes, maybe if you'd given that one last hug, maybe been available for one last phone call, maybe called the doctor one more time, maybe this wouldn't have happened— at this time. And maybe not. If the road to hell is paved with good intentions, its road signs are the maybe's of our lives.

If you feel anger toward others as well, you're normal. You wish you could have rescued your loved one, and you wish others would have saved her. That's how much you loved—be grateful for that.

In time, you should feel free of the anger you might naturally feel toward her. "How could you do this to me—to us?" becomes "I'm so sorry you were *this* sick, *this* desperate."

Expect little of yourself for the time being.

Pamper your body, your mind, your soul until you feel healing begin.

Accept that some answers may never come, not on this earth.

You feel at such a loss because your loved one cannot give any answers now. If addiction to drugs or alcohol was the basis for the suicide, it was also the basis for an irrational decision.

If a lengthy struggle with depression preceded the death, you must grant your loved one the autonomy to have known when enough was enough. Only he could know.

Note progress:

"Today I got out of bed."

"Today I took a shower."

"Today I could eat without knots in my stomach."

Find and read some literature of rage.

For instance, Psalms 13, 22, 61, 64, 77, 88, and 102 may help you rail against this injustice which has turned your world upside down. *No one* has ever felt quite as you do now, but the writers of these psalms express similar anger, depression, and isolation. They can help you give voice to your feelings, and they bestow deep peace and comfort as well.

Now may be time to begin finalizing your memories.

At least think of collecting materials for assembling a collage, scrapbook, or special photo album. This activity may be painful, but it is also, as part of your grief work, very therapeutic.

Consider planning a special service to commemorate your loved one's life.

Even if you didn't have one earlier, the process of creating and participating in a special observance is still healing.

Too, the support of friends and family is still needed, and this provides an opportunity for them to show it.

Affirm what is good in yourself.

This is called self-healing.

RECUPERATION

Affirm what is good in others.

This is called *love*, the greatest healer of all.

Surround yourself with light.

Open drapes and blinds during the day. Turn on lights at night.

Let the power of light heal the darkness in your soul.

More layers of your being are "learning" (and accepting) that your loved one is gone.

Each recollection of a shared moment pricks the bittersweet bonds of memory. In time these should soothe your sense of loss rather than aggravate it.

Time may still be distorted for you.

This is probably due mostly to poor concentration.

For many, time shortens, especially when they're alone. You may find yourself thinking about this horrible event so often that your thoughts almost become an obsession. What may seem like a few minutes may in fact be an hour when you're in this mode.

The opposite can happen as well when time drags and a few minutes are perceived as an hour. Some day your clock will return to normal. Trust it.

The "anniversary" of your loved one's death may exacerbate the grieving process.

Just thinking of the day of the week may cause you to re-live those horrible hours. In time, Wednesdays (or whatever day) will be more like the rest of the week.

Don't despair if the usual things that give you comfort or pleasure now fail to uplift.

Let them back in
                    bit

                                by

                                        bit.

Visit "The Recovery Room" (or "The Emergency Room") as often as needed.

Understanding will gradually come, if not full explanations.

The vast majority of suicides result from prolonged depression, a state which by its very nature, alters rational thinking. One has been sucked into a whirlpool so long that nothing but the pain and exhaustion of the struggle is real.

Whether being treated or not, symptoms can become demons that overwhelm all judgment and objectivity. Your loved one could not share these unimaginably painful feelings with you or with anyone. To talk about them would have made them even more painfully real.

If your loved one appeared to be getting better, it may be that having a plan to relieve suffering gave her peace of mind. Experts say this is fairly common. Those in treatment, especially as the course of treatment nears a close, are sometimes the most vulnerable.

Decision-making will still be difficult.

Even in the small matters of life, you may find yourself drawing constant blanks.

One woman, several weeks after her husband's suicide, could not decide whether to buy white or yellow American cheese.

So she bought both.

It's okay to feel grateful and relieved that your loved one's suffering has ended.

Such feelings can co-exist without destroying your mental health.

Plan for anniversaries.

Whether they are birthdays, wedding anniversaries, holiday celebrations, or the anniversary of the death, give them special attention.

Your plan might include:

- a visit to the cemetery,

- inviting a friend in to reminisce

- buying yourself (or somebody else) flowers,

- a visit to relatives or friends to share recollections of happier times,

- planning an event not particularly related to your loved one to honor the memory in a conscious way.

The sting will be less painful if you think ahead of time of ways to observe special occasions.

Keep writing.

Keep talking.

Keep breathing.

Reminders of your loved one will be bittersweet for a long time.

Such memories have a beauty of their own. Let them decorate your life as much as you wish. If personal belongings such as clothing, books, and other reminders, like photographs, are too painful, put them aside. Don't throw anything away yet; you may want to "visit" them later.

Let familiar items bring comfort. One woman slept with her husband's robe. Another kept her son's sweatshirt (unwashed), another her son's toddler-teddy bear, and another mourner kept the loved one's small personal items in a special drawer. You will notice when such things no longer comfort. If they become a problem, store them until you decide if you want to dispose of them.

Photographs can be a mixed blessing, evoking painful reminders but also bringing comfort for the connectedness they represent. If not now, one day they will be treasured.

Slowly learn ways to cope.

Develop strategies helpful to you, whether it's new aspects of daily living you must tackle on your own or new ways to handle your emotions. Many excellent books are available to help you deal with grief and loneliness.

If by now you think you might benefit from talking with a therapist or clergyman, by all means, seek someone out. Ask your physician or friends for recommendations. Remember that it takes strength, not weakness, to recognize when you need help. Ask for it.

Find a support group.

Bereavement groups for survivors exist in many areas, even specifically for survivors of the aftermath of suicide. By now, you realize that suicide bereavement is in a class different from that caused by other kinds of deaths.

People have benefitted from suicide survivor's support groups as long as thirty years after their loved ones' deaths and found comfort. One mother became a recluse twenty-five years ago when her son took his life. Self-help groups did not exist in her area then so of course she never attended any.

Don't let this happen to you.

Still angry?

If you are—with your loved one, with others, with yourself, with God—pray for peace of mind and the ability to forgive.

If you need to vent your anger, find a safe place to pound a pillow, yell, or throw things.

Never vent on a person.

Re-reading sympathy cards and notes may be helpful.

You appreciated the thoughts behind them when they arrived but were probably numb then. Now their messages may be even more meaningful.

Use friends well in this period of healing.

They ache for you and sometimes don't know how to help. Let them know how to help. Let them know if what you want is a visit—short, please!—or a phone call or a casserole.

You may not be ready for social events for months. Such effort can be exhausting. Now you need energy just to get well. Everyone can understand that and be patient with you if you're still recuperating.

If you do go to an event, it's best to drive your own car in case you want to leave early.

Begin to set achievable goals.

One or two a day will be enough at first. (Getting out of bed may be one of them.)

Praise yourself for progress.

Deal with regret and guilt as needed.

If they continue to plague you, admit that perhaps you may have made mistakes in your relationship with your loved one (if that seems to be the case). But why do you think you should have been perfect? Remember gratefully the loving things you did do.

It's very painful to realize you were unable to help your loved one out of the last morass. You are forced to acknowledge your own weakness and vulnerability. It hurts to know you are only human.

Because we are human beings, we have imperfect natures. This means we all are self-centered at least some of the time.

Forgive yourself for not being perfect.

To know what forgiveness feels like, you can use your imagination.

Picture yourself standing in a refreshing shower. Watch the water wash your sweat and grime and weariness down the drain. Feel the water make you clean and whole and new again.

(You can take a real shower, too.)

Know this miracle that water—and God—can perform. Rejoice!

You may "see" your loved one.

She's walking down the street or passing in a car. You see her shape, her clothing, the set of her head, even her face.

These momentary flashbacks can startle you and make you question your sanity. They are normal memory connections, however, which survivors often experience. Find solace in them as you realize how very deep those connections are.

Visit your doctor when necessary.

Your physical self has been assaulted by this tragedy just as much as your emotional, mental, and spiritual selves have. Deal with symptoms while they are still minor.

Begin to reconcile ambivalent feelings.

Guilt, anger, relief, forgiveness, and other hard emotions jar when sitting next to each other, seemingly occupying the same space. Yet it is part of being human to claim opposite feelings at the same time.

A wise man once said that it's a mark of maturity to learn to live with ambivalent feelings. Simultaneous opposite emotions are a reflection of this contradictory world we inhabit, and holding them means you're doing more than hanging on.

Welcome and use music.

No matter what your tastes are, music can uplift or help you get in touch with sad feelings. (Remember how you deferred some of your crying while you were in the Emergency Room?)

Appreciate the beauty of both—your feelings and the music.

By now you realize that your life has changed forever.

Note: It has changed, not ended.

Don't be afraid to visit the Land of the Truth.

When you're ready, whatever your personal feelings are, own them. Whatever you can find out about the suicide, face it. It's the only way to be real.

Indulge in sorrow as much as you need to.

If feelings of sadness become too uncomfortable, call a friend, mow the yard, volunteer your services, do what you need to do for diversion.

Begin to reach out to others.

Even if their needs are different from yours, becoming more sensitive to others will help prevent your pain from overwhelming you.

Keep telling your story.

Repetition makes the truth more real. If your friends tire of hearing it, find those who will listen, such as a counselor or support group. Even using a tape recorder may be helpful.

And don't forget to "talk" to your journal.

Don't isolate yourself.

Alone-ness is inevitable if the missing loved one was a spouse. Loneliness is not. You don't have to be a part of the conspiracy of silence against grieving that society exacts upon mourners.

Seek out ways to develop or enrich your faith.

God's grace heals and empowers you as it helps you find your center.

Even if you've heretofore not found religion to be meaningful, now it may provide comfort that can be found no other way. Any house of worship will welcome you, but you may be more comfortable attending with a friend or family member. Just ask.

If you seek a private way to get in touch with God, perhaps in addition to worship, many helpful devotional materials can be found in bookstores.

Don't forget to pray. God listens, especially to those in pain.

Begin to chart a new course for yourself.

You are now in this world without your loved one. Especially if she was a spouse, many sudden overwhelming changes have been thrust upon you. You have to "re-invent" yourself as well as create a new life. It's a scary adventure to be sure, but one which promises new kinds of freedoms eventually. However, don't make any important life changes—moving, new job, marriage—for at least a year.

Self-confidence suffers with any major loss. Eventually you may want to nurture its re-building. If you give thought to a self-improvement plan, such as Weight Watchers or Assertiveness Training, follow through with it, but *only* if it makes you feel good about yourself.

The last thing you need is goal-setting that will make you feel like a failure if you don't meet it. Now you just need to heal.

Grief washes over you in waves.

You may think recuperation is well under way when a fresh surge of sadness and depression hits. Ride with it, if you can. Get help to battle the waves if they're too high, if eating and sleeping patterns are greatly interrupted, or if low concentration levels or motivation are affecting your ability to function.

This ebb and flow may continue for many, many months. Like the surf rider, look up and ahead rather than down. This may mean special planning for a future event or activity for yourself so that anticipation can help lift you out of the trough.

Turn negative internal dialogue into positive.

If you feel like a failure, your language not only reflects but reinforces a defeated attitude.

It may take tremendous effort, but it will pay off for you to change "I can't," "I don't," and "I'm not" into "I *can*" and "I *will*." Your emotional outlook will change too.

Above all, ban "what if" and "if only" from your vocabulary.

Question God if you need to.

Moses did, so did Jonah, even Jesus. Job learned that God not only accepted uncomfortable questions but honored them as well. Many figures of the Old and New Testaments as well as giants of other sacred and secular literature have wrestled with God in the midst of life crises.

Honor God with your honesty, no matter what it's made of. Trust enough to give God your doubt, anger, confusion, guilt, your questions of any nature. When truthful with God and with ourselves, and especially when we admit vulnerability, we can find God in the midst of the struggle, creating an intimate bond. God cannot be in relationship with us otherwise.

You might even find God weeping tears along with you. God's love is that strong and that real.

Respect your need to take life one step at a time.

Your best coping strategy will be to take a day or an hour at a time, for as long as you need to.

This takes courage, especially when your whole being wants to give up.

Time heals, but not by itself. Talk heals, but not by itself. Tears heal, but not by themselves.

There is a sweet mystery in the process of healing. It has been taking place in your body, your mind, and your soul. This process will continue.

Believe—and lean into it.

You may eventually find some answers.

They will always be multiple and complex, never definitive to your "why's." some may come from reading, meeting with other suicide survivors, talking and journaling about your own perceptions, and perhaps counseling. Causes of your loved one's death will always partially remain an enigma, as are circumstances surrounding many deaths.

Accepting this truth may be the hardest choice you will make. To choose otherwise is to live with rage, fear, and guilt that will destroy both you and those around you.

Make a contract with yourself.

It's important to make a personal commitment to persist in your recovery plan.

Write and sign it in your journal or do it right here, right now:

On this _____ day of _____, I pledge that I *will* survive.

This is my survival plan:

_____

_____

_____

_____

This is one of the worst kinds of death to grieve through, and you're surviving it.

As you gain perspective on this sorrow, it won't consume you anymore. In ordinary daylight, you are beginning to grow your life around it.

Will you be changed? Absolutely!

Will your faith be re-shaped? Most certainly!

For better or for worse? Believe it or not, it's your option. Get all the help you can to say yes to life again.

Please continue breathing. Deeply.

Part of breathing is called inspiration, or "Spirit coming into." Let Spirit come.

You made it this far.

You will survive.

Made in the USA
Middletown, DE
04 March 2019